It Depends On How You Look At It!

It Depends On How You Look At It!

Rusty Bolton

A Key to Practical Christian Living

foreword by
Paul Faulkner

Christian Communications
P.O. Box 150
Nashville, TN 37202

Copyrighted © 1989 by Gospel Advocate Co.

All rights reserved. No part of this publication may be reproduced, stored in a retrieval system, or transmitted in any form or by any means—electronic, mechanical, photocopy, recording, or any other—except for brief quotations in printed reviews, without the prior permission of the publisher.

IT IS ILLEGAL AND UNETHICAL TO DUPLICATE COPYRIGHTED MATERIAL.

The material in this study represents a considerable investment in effort, skill, time, and finances from both the author and the publisher. If this material is photocopied and circulated to avoid buying a book for each student, the author is defrauded of duly earned royalties, and the publisher does not sell enough copies to support the publication.

Christian Communications is a division of the Gospel Advocate Co., P.O. Box 150, Nashville, TN 37202

ISBN 0-89225-358-4

Second Printing, June 1990

*I lovingly dedicate this book to my wife, Martha,
whose deep faith in God gives me strength,
whose confidence in me gives me security,
whose gentle femininity gives me pleasure,
whose delightful spirit gives me joy.*

*"The lamp of the body is the eye; if therefore your eye is clear, your whole body will be full of light.
But, if your eye is bad, your whole body will be full of darkness."*

Matthew 6:22-23

CONTENTS

Page

MY PERSONAL LIFE
1. You Can be in Control 3
2. What Am I For? 11
3. The Normal Christian Life 21
4. When Things Are Tough 29
5. The Power of a Dream 38

MY LIFE WITH OTHERS
6. Making Your Marriage Sparkle 49
7. What About Me, I'm Single? 60
8. Does It Work for Teens, Too? 69
9. Fitting into the Church 79

MY LIFE WITH GOD
10. Seeing What God Is Doing 89
11. God at Work in My Life 96

FOREWORD

Rusty's book is good. He is a good, clear writer.

The title states the basic premise: we cannot control what happens to us. There are many points that cause the reader to stop and think.

Bolton has the ability to focus on one point and make that point with clarity and accuracy. He does a good job of explaining some important psychological information in basic terms that are easily understood.

His philosophical orientation is very biblical, focusing on the fact that life is purposeful. I recommend it.

Paul B. Faulkner, Ed.D.
Abilene Christian University

INTRODUCTION

My son Danny was not known as a scholar. Bright, precocious, delightful and a "ham," but not a scholar.

You can imagine my surprise when, as a freshman in college, he announced that he had discovered the *secret to life*. He knew the secret of making life successful. "In fact," he said, "I'm thinking about getting me a mountain and becoming a guru so people can climb up and ask, 'Oh, Great One, what is the secret to life?'"

My interest peaked, and I asked, "Tell me, Danny, what have you discovered? What *is* the secret to life?" He answered, "It depends on how you look at it."

I started to laugh; then I realized that he was on target. People everywhere were trying to keep their lives right side up and make it make sense to them. And Danny had discovered a basic key that is needed. Happy, successful, functional individuals and families all have problems. Some people simply choose to view their problems differently, and that makes all the difference.

Of course, others have discovered the same truth. It is the basis of cognitive psychotherapy. Stated another way, it would be, "Control the way you choose to view things, and you control your destiny."

Introduction

Jesus said it this way: "The lamp of the body is the eye; if therefore your eye is clear, your whole body will be full of light. But, if your eye is bad, your whole body will be full of darkness" (Matthew 6:22-23).

Paul, the Apostle, used these words, "To the pure, all things are pure; but to those who are defiled and unbelieving, nothing is pure, but both their mind and their conscience are defiled" (Titus 1:15).

In other words, Danny was right. A significant secret to life is this: It depends on how you look at it.

Using this premise, we will take another look at ourselves, our lives with others, and our lives with God.

One word of caution: while this is a valid, biblical principle that we can use to help us be more victorious, it can be misunderstood and misused. This principle, if overstated, could become a humanistic attempt to pull ourselves up by our own bootstraps. Nothing could be more impossible. God is God, Jesus is His Son, and His Way is best in every situation. That is true, no matter what we believe. It would be true even if we were never born.

Here's the point: the glorious, transcendent power and wisdom of God is available to us. It can transform our lives. But, before we can appropriate it to our lives, we must see it and respond to it. Our view—the way we choose to look at it—is of crucial importance.

MY PERSONAL LIFE

CHAPTER 1

You Can Be in Control

Many people feel like a Ping-Pong ball on a West Texas parking lot where the wind blows. Their view of life at any moment is determined by what is happening to them and around them. If the wind blows one way and things around them are doing well, then they can be happy and cheerful. If it happens to blow another way, and things around them are difficult or painful, then they must be unhappy and depressed. Outside factors dictate their mood. They have little control.

Other people seem to have found a handle to life and can even choose to go against the wind. Even when things are going particularly bad, they can remain optimistic, cheerful and in control.

Actually, every day of your life there are real reasons to be depressed, and there are real reasons to be positive and cheerful. How your day goes depends on which reasons you choose to focus on.

It depends on how you look at it.

We Are Constantly Responsible

Each person is responsible and accountable for his attitudes and behavior all the time. There is never an occasion when you can act improperly and blame someone else.

In the 1950's television sit-com "The Real McCoys," Walter Brennan played Grandpa McCoy. He would often make blunders which led to comical predicaments. However, he never accepted responsibility for the blunders. He would typically turn to another member of the family and say, "See what *you* made me do!"

Blaming others for our attitudes and behavior is the oldest trick in the Book. In the Garden of Eden God had told Adam and Eve not to eat the fruit of the tree of knowledge of good and evil. The serpent tempted Eve, and she ate. Then she offered some to Adam, and he ate.

When God confronted the first man with the first sin, Adam, in true, manly fashion, blamed it on his wife. In essence he said, "I'm not responsible for what I did because, you see, I was tempted. Eve is responsible for my behavior." Eve followed suit and blamed her sin on the serpent. Of course, the serpent didn't have a leg to stand on.

Even though they both explained that they were not responsible, God said, in effect, "You must leave the garden because you *are always* responsible for your behavior." That's true even when you're tempted. Even when you have a headache. Even when you're rushed. Even when you're tired. Even . . . even . . . even.

That's true because one person cannot make another do anything he chooses not to do—good or bad. You cannot make me yell at you, if I choose not to. You cannot make me be warm and friendly, if I choose not to be. You may make it more difficult for me to act a certain way, but whatever you do, I have several alternative ways to respond. And I am responsible for the response I choose to make.

A Sign of Maturity

You don't have to act the way you feel. You can feel one way and choose to act another. The only creature on earth that can do that is an adult human being. Infants can't. Animals can't.

Recently, my son Jeff and his wife Pam gave birth to a precious baby girl. When they brought her home from the hospital, she would wake up in the middle of the night, as babies do. She didn't lay there

> *Each person is responsible and accountable for his attitudes and behavior all the time. There is never an occasion when you can act improperly and blame someone else.*

and think, "Mom's had a hard day, and she just got out of the hospital. She needs her sleep; so, I'll just lie here quietly and wait until she wakes up and checks on me." No, infants can only *act* the way they *feel*. A sign of maturity is when a person begins to act from thought instead of feelings alone. As Amy grows up, she will discover this.

Why would I ever want to believe that something or someone else is responsible for my behavior? Because, if that's true, then I have no guilt and no responsibility to change. It's really someone else's fault, and I'm just a helpless victim.

Unowned Behavior

One sure tip-off that someone is avoiding responsibility is when they express *unowned behavior*. That is, behavior they exhibited but refuse to "own". We use phrases like these:

"I *lost* my temper," instead of saying, "I chose to act stupidly." We pretend that our temper is something we can inadvertently misplace—like our car keys.

"I don't know *what* came over me." In other words, something else for which I'm not responsible took charge of me for a while.

"That isn't like me."

"I was beside myself."

We will go to almost any length to avoid responsibility. We blame our mates, parents, children, bosses, jobs, environment, car problems, health, circumstances, society, vitamin shortages, or anything else that comes to mind.

Deep inside, though, we know that there ought to be a way to live responsibly in a messed-up world. We all have to live with imperfect mates and bring up imperfect kids. We live near imperfect neighbors and have imperfect bosses. We attend a church with imperfect folks and listen to imperfect preachers. The glorious good news is that we don't *ever* have to respond wrongly—even when things go particularly bad, and even when we have been maliciously wronged. Isn't that great!

It depends on how you look at it.

It's Your Choice

Dr. David Augsburger is one of the leading authorities on anger in this country. I went to an anger workshop taught by him to mental health professionals. He began by showing an overhead picture of a little man standing under a tree. The tree had no leaves on it. He was standing under the tree, leaning on a rake beside a huge pile of leaves. He obviously had worked for over an hour raking them. The picture showed a cat behind him being chased by several dogs heading straight for the pile of leaves. They were about to scatter the pile of leaves he had worked so hard to rake.

As we looked at the picture, Dr. Augsburger asked, "What do you think will be this little man's reaction when the leaves are scattered?"

Knowing that we were at an anger workshop, we began answering, "anger," "hostility," "frustration," and every synonym we could think of for anger. Each time Dr. Augsburger would say, "Yes, anything else?"

Finally, an insightful lady said, "Delight. He will be delighted. When the leaves scatter it will remind him of when he used to play in the leaves as a boy. He will roll and tumble with glee."

That was Dr. Augsburger's point. As long as he viewed the inevitable scattering of leaves as a terrible injustice, then his reaction would be anger. If he

---

You don't have to act the way you feel.

---

chose to reframe it and see it as an opportunity to play, then his reaction would be delight.

It depended on how he looked at it.

Suppose you are in a nearby shopping mall. It's crowded. You're in a hurry. You have noticed some rather rowdy teenagers at the mall and wondered why their parents allowed them to "hang out" there.

As you are walking briskly with your packages, you catch a glimpse from the corner of your eye of someone approaching you. Then, that person jams a stick between your feet and trips you. You fall ungracefully to the floor, dropping your packages, aware of people stopping and staring.

How do you feel? Be very sensitive to your feelings at this moment. What do you feel like doing?

At this point you look up and see a little grey-haired lady who is blind. She has accidently tripped you with her cane. She is now aware that she has

---

Losers blame other people and circumstances and continue to fail. Winners have the same situations to deal with, but they choose to view them differently, retain control and responsibility, and they overcome.

---

done something awful. She's trembling a little and beginning to cry.

Now, how do you feel? Have your feelings changed? What do you feel like doing now?

Notice what changed. Not the situation. It remained the same. The only difference was the way you interpreted it.

It depends on how you look at it. And, this amazing power is available to you in *every* situation of life.

Taught Throughout the Bible

Characters in the Bible show this principle over and over.

The Israelites were wandering in the wilderness. They could have looked forward to the Promised Land and the care of God (as Joshua and Caleb did). This would have brought anticipation and victory.

Instead, they chose to look backward to Egypt, which caused them to perish in the wilderness.

Jesus taught in the Sermon on the Mount that it is not only wrong to commit adultery or murder, but it becomes wrong *before* that—"in the heart" (Matthew 5:27-28).

No matter how Jesus might have felt when beaten and crucified, He still chose to say, "Father, forgive them" (Luke 23:34).

Paul and Silas, after being wrongly arrested, beaten and thrown in the inner prison, chose to "pray and sing hymns of praise to God" (Acts 16:25).

Losers blame other people and circumstances and continue to fail. Winners have the same situations to deal with, but they choose to view them differently, retain control and responsibility, and they overcome.

Questions for Thought and Discussion

1. When have you felt like a Ping-Pong ball in a windy parking lot?
2. Whom have you known that, despite real adversity, chose to be positive and cheerful? Do you know someone who sees gloom and doom without real reason?
3. Do you agree that there is never an occasion to act improperly and blame someone else? Explain. When are you most tempted to do so?
4. Why do we want to believe that someone or something else is to blame for our improper behavior?
5. What is *unowned behavior*? Give some examples.
6. Think of a time when you chose to "reframe" a situation and, thus, changed your attitude toward it?
7. What situation or relationship in your life now could be improved if you chose to view it differently?

CHAPTER 2

What Am I For?

Would you believe me if I told you that no one in the city of Memphis will be allowed to vote in the Tennessee state elections, or in the national American elections?

Would you believe me if I told you that two plus two do *not* equal four?

Both statements are true.

In Egypt there is a city named Memphis. People in that city are not citizens of Tennessee or the U.S.A. and, therefore, will not be allowed to vote in their elections.

If we use the base ten system, as we ordinarily do, two plus two equals four. But, if we switch to a base three system there is no "four," and in that system two plus two is one-one (or eleven).

> *The Christian enjoys pleasure. But that's not what he's for.*

Before we can understand each other, we must have the same premise, the same framework. Otherwise, nothing seems to make sense. Christians and

11

non-Christians often fail to understand each other because they operate with different premises.

The Basis for All Behavior

People behave differently. Sometimes the behavior is inconsequential, and sometimes it is significant. Sometimes it is moral, sometimes it is immoral, and sometimes it is amoral. We decide what to have for breakfast, and we decide whether to be faithful to our mate. We decide what color socks to wear, and we decide whether to serve God or not. Our behavior is pictured as the outer circle on the following Figure A.

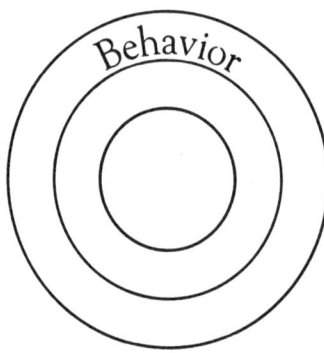

Figure A

But, our behavior is *based* on something. Why do we behave the way we do? Our behavior is based on our *values*. (See Figure B.) Behaviors differ from one person to another because we have different values. One person places high value on a new sports car; so his behavior differs from one who doesn't. The values we put on money, fame, God, Christian family, looks, health, education, etc., determine our behavior.

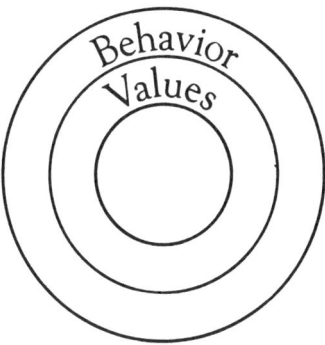

Figure B

Our values are based on something, too. Why do we have the values we have? Our values are based on our *world view*. (See Figure C.) That's basic. What is this world? Where did it come from? What is the nature of man? Does God exist? What is life for? What is a human being for?

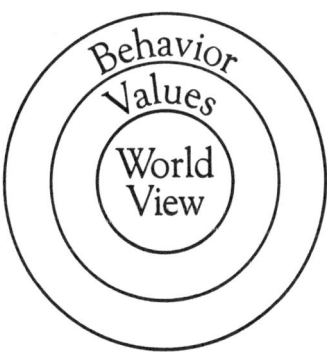

Figure C

Everyone is for something. A fork is for eating. A shovel is for digging in the earth. And they work. If we get them mixed, though, and try to dig up the garden with a table fork or eat with a garden shovel, it won't work. Why? Because that's not what they are for.

What is a human being for? What are you for?

When you answer those questions, you will know your world view, which determines your values, which determine your behavior.

Two World Views

Basically, there are two world views in our culture. You have probably bought into one or the other.

> *One thing you cannot do is keep a Christian from glorifying God. That's his nature. That's who he is. Torture him if you will. Kill him if you must. He will only glorify God in his persecution and death.*

There is the non-Christian world view and the Christian world view. They are vastly different.

1. *The Non-Christian World View*

For the non-Christian, the purpose of life basically is to find pleasure. He marshals his time, energy and resources toward that end. At the basis of each decision are these questions: "What would I like best? Which would I prefer?" The more pleasure he finds and the more displeasure he avoids, the more successful his life.

Ernest Hemingway is reported to have defined *moral* as, "what you feel good after."

This world view can be seen by looking at the Roman arena when Christians were thrown to lions. The Romans, who believed the purpose of life was pleasure, could simply not understand those stupid Christians. There was certainly no pleasure in being killed by a lion. All they had to do to be freed was to say, "Caesar is Lord." But they wouldn't do it! And, to the Romans, it just didn't make sense.

2. *The Christian World View*

The Christian enjoys pleasure. And he doesn't like displeasure. But that's not what he's for. That's not his purpose of life. For the Christian, the purpose of life is to glorify God. He marshals his time, energy and resources toward that end. At the basis of each decision are these questions: "What will bring more honor to God? What would *He* have me do?" When the will of God is involved, pleasure has nothing to do with it.

The Christian is aware of Ecclesiastes 12:13: "This is the end of the matter. All has been heard. Fear God and keep His commandments, for this is the whole duty of man."

He is fond of Colossians 3:17 which reads, "Whatever you do in word or deed, do all in the name of the Lord. . . ."

One thing you cannot do is keep a Christian from glorifying God. That's his nature. That's who he is. Torture him if you will. Kill him if you must. He will only glorify God in his persecution and in his death.

It must also be pointed out that the Christians in the arena didn't understand the Romans either.

The Christians knew the purpose of life was to glorify God. What those Romans were doing was an affront to Him. "How can they do that? Don't they know how God must feel?" Even though they couldn't understand the Romans, they died with a song of praise to God on their lips and a quiet confidence that silently said, "I know something you don't know!"

There continues to be a clash between these two world views. There always has been. There always will be. Jesus predicted it. He said, "If you were of the world, the world would love its own; but because you are not of the world, but I chose you out of the world, therefore the world hates you" (John 15:19).

Trying to Do Right for Wrong Reasons

The problem is that Christians are constantly tempted to justify their behaviors and lifestyles by the non-Christian world view. We try to point out that faithfully serving the Lord brings more *pleasure*.

We advertise our youth rallies by saying that they will be *fun*. We ask people to join Bible study groups because they will *enjoy* it. Singles are urged to attend a special retreat because it will *meet their needs*.

Why are we tempted to go back to the pleasure principle, the non-Christian world view, to justify our activities? I think there are two major reasons.

It's All Around Us

First, our culture is based on the pleasure principle. We are surrounded by it and immersed in it. We accept it by osmosis. Almost every television program we watch, song we hear, magazine we read, and movie we attend is based on the non-Christian world view.

Just consider the incidents of drunkenness, adultery, homosexuality, and other non-Christian activities depicted in an average day on television. And note that they are depicted as "normal."

Even the good "family" shows have the non-Christian world view at their base. I remember seeing an episode of "Family Ties" where Mallory, a teenage girl, was having to decide whether to have sex with her boyfriend. She discussed it with her boyfriend, her girlfriends, her brother, and her parents, but none had an answer for her. The non-Christian world view had no answer for Mallory, nor for the millions of other teenage girls faced with the same decision.

The television industry claims to only *reflect* modern culture and not *set* our values. However, it does *not* accurately reflect our culture. You never see a happy, healthy, Christian family who has Jesus at the center of their lives—even though 60 percent of Americans claim to be Christians. Perhaps television is called a *medium* because it is neither rare nor well-done.

Where Do You Draw the Line?

A second reason Christians are tempted to revert to the pleasure principle is because many decisions are appropriately based there. Many decisions are amoral—neither right nor wrong. Do you want orange juice or apple juice for breakfast? Do you want to drive a Ford or a Chevrolet? Since the will of God allows either choice, it is appropriate to decide on the basis of pleasure or personal preference.

Because there are so many valid decisions made on that basis, it's difficult to know where to draw the line. Basically, when the will of God is involved, then pleasure becomes secondary or invalid. Christians always honor God. That's what they are for.

Even from the Pulpit

Ironically, much preaching is done in an attempt to justify Christianity by the non-Christian world view. It's as though we are saying, "Sure, our purpose is to find pleasure, but in the long run, the Christian lifestyle brings more pleasure."

We point out, for instance, that following Christian principles will help you avoid alcoholism and drug addiction. We imply that is why you should be a Christian. We point out that by following Christian principles you will most likely have a happy, stable home. And, again, we imply that is why you should be a Christian.

> *If God chooses to bless you with health and prosperity, that's fine—praise Him! If He chooses that you should be thrown to the lions, that's fine, too—praise Him!*

While both are generally true, *that is not why* you should be a Christian! You should be a Christian even if it brings persecution and death.

While it is *generally* true that living by Christian principles brings more pleasure, it is not *always* true.

During the Roman persecution, there was no pleasure—short or long run—in this life in being dragged through the streets by a running horse instead of denying the faith. But it was still the right decision to hold on to that faith.

Even today I know some people who remain in difficult marriages, not because it brings personal pleasure, but because God is honored by so doing. Some remain in difficult church situations when there is precious little personal joy because it is God's will in their life.

When the will of God is involved, pleasure is not the motivation.

Christians must recognize the clear, fundamental difference between the two world views. We must live a life that is consistent with our world view—expecting to be misunderstood.

When we understand this clear clash between fundamental world views, some favorite scriptures take on new meanings:

"I am crucified with Christ, nevertheless I live, yet not I, but Christ lives in me" (Galatians 2:20).

"But God be thanked that though you were slaves to sin . . . you became slaves to righteousness" (Romans 6:17-18).

"Do not be conformed to this world, but be transformed by the renewing of your mind, that you may prove what the will of God is, that which is good and acceptable and perfect" (Romans 12:20).

"Do you not know that your body is the temple of the Holy Spirit who is in you, whom you have from God, and that you are not your own? For you have been bought with a price, therefore, glorify God in your body" (1 Corinthians 6:19-20).

Summary

Sometimes the behavior of the world and the behavior of the Christian are compatible. They don't *always* clash. But, even then, they spring from two entirely different sources and *will often clash*.

The Christian has settled the basic questions of who he is and Whose he is. He does right simply because it is right—no other reason. Whether it is fun or pleasant has nothing to do with it.

Then, if God chooses to bless you with health and prosperity, that's fine—praise Him! If he chooses that you should be thrown to the lions, that's fine, too—praise Him!

Questions for Thought and Discussion

1. Distinguish between behavior, values and world view.
2. What are the two world views common in our culture? How do they differ and why?
3. Give examples of Christians attempting to justify their behavior by the non-Christian world view.
4. Why do you think modern movies and television fail to reflect that portion of our culture with a Christian world view? What effect is this having?
5. Is it ever appropriate to consider your own desires and your own pleasure in making a decision?
6. Does living by Christian principles always bring more pleasure in our culture?
7. Give an example of a Christian being misunderstood by others when making a decision that honored God. Can Christians expect to be misunderstood?

CHAPTER 3

The Normal Christian Life

No one wants to be abnormal.

One of the least complimentary things you can say about someone is, "He's nice, but he's a little strange."

Our children learn that early. One of their most persuasive arguments to get parents to purchase some item is, "Everybody's got one." This implies that if he doesn't get one he'll be abnormal. And we certainly can't have that!

The only reason I wear a necktie is to look normal. It doesn't keep me warm like my coat. It doesn't protect me like my shoes. It just hangs there. I wear it because in some situations it is *normally* expected. And I don't want to be abnormal.

In the last chapter we pointed out that Christians serve God without considering whether it is pleasurable or not. That is a good and important principle. Like all principles, though, it can be misunderstood.

Because one submits totally to God, some have the idea that living as a Christian is difficult, and dreary, and terribly abnormal. In fact, in a conversation recently, a sincere man said to me, "I'd like to be a Christian, but I'm afraid I couldn't live a normal life any more."

Living as you were designed by your Designer is the most normal thing you can do. Anything else would be out of harmony with the character and nature of God.

Consistent with God's Design

God created fish. He placed within them the need and the desire to swim through the waters and be free. Wouldn't it have been cruel and out of character for a wise, loving God to design fish with that need and desire and then paralyze them so they couldn't swim as they were designed? God didn't do that to fish.

God created birds. He placed within them the need and the desire to fly and to soar through the heavens. Wouldn't it have been cruel and out of character for a wise, loving God to design birds with that need and desire, and then make their wings unable to do what they were designed to do? God didn't do that to birds.

God created man. He placed within him the need and desire to enjoy life and be free. Wouldn't it have been cruel and out of character for a wise, loving God to design man with that need and desire, and then command him to live in a way that is unnatural and contrary to his design? God didn't do that to man.

Life's Greatest Serendipity

Christianity is life's greatest serendipity. The word "serendipity" was coined by Sir Horace Walpole in 1754. He wrote about the three princes of Serendip (modern-day Cambodia). These princes were so attuned to life that they found great unexpected adventures while on journeys for their king. The word came to mean, "the gift of finding unexpected valuable things while searching for something else."

Life is filled with serendipities.

Sir Alexander Fleming in 1929 was researching influenza. He had a culture plate of staphylococcus germs under his microscope. A gust of wind blew through an open window scattering some dust around. After closing the window, he noticed that a speck of dust had blown onto his culture plate. His first thought was that the experiment was ruined. He looked again and noticed a bacteria-free circle around the dust speck. He found it actually to be a speck of mold and, thus, began the research that resulted in the discovery of penicillin.

Columbus did not set out to discover America. He was looking for something else entirely. He was looking for a new trade route to China.

You can surely think of several serendipities in your life. Perhaps, it is how you met your mate. You didn't go out that day looking for someone to marry,

> *You don't have to give up one single thing that's good for you in order to be a Christian.*

but you were attuned to possibilities. Perhaps, how you got into your career was a serendipity.

Life's greatest serendipity is found in Matthew 6:33, "Seek ye first the kingdom of God, and His righteousness, and all these things will be added unto you."

If you attempt to find joy, peace and happiness, you will not find them. They don't come that way. It's unnatural. Those qualities come as a by-product, or serendipity, of serving God.

What About Tense Christians?

If that is true, and Christianity brings inner peace and joy, why are there so many tense, unhappy, religious fanatics?

There are always the unbalanced who seek the extreme in every area of life.

In politics, some go beyond a normal and appropriate concern about the spread of communism. They see a communist plot behind every public utterance.

In race relations, some go to unreasonable extremes and think that everyone of a certain ethnic group is bad or good.

In sports, some are fanatical. One man recently said to his wife, "Now, honey, is there anything you want to say to me before baseball season starts?"

Since religion is a basic part of life, it is not surprising that it attracts its share of extremists and fanatics. But that is not the spirit of the New Testament or a result of properly following Christ.

Jesus is our example: He "kept increasing in wisdom and stature, and in favor with God and men" (Luke 2:52).

One of the first descriptions of early Christians describes them "praising God, and having favor with all the people" (Acts 2:47).

The fruit of the Spirit is "love, joy, peace, patience, kindness, goodness, faithfulness, gentleness, self-control" (Galatians 5:22-23).

Christians are commanded, "If possible, so far as it depends on you, be at peace with all men" (Romans 12:18).

We Christians are to so live that, even if folks think we believe weird things, they will be impressed with what we have—fulfilled, joyous, peaceable lives.

What About All I Will Have To Give Up?

Someone asks, "What about all the fun things that I'll have to give up if I become a Christian?" That's a fair question and a common understanding. When I was growing up in the farming town of Dos Palos, California, that was my understanding. To me, Christianity was a long list of a lot of fun things that Christians weren't supposed to do.

I don't know where the idea came from. Perhaps it came from a rumor. Perhaps it came from warped religionists. But it did not come from the Bible. You don't have to give up one single thing that's good for you in order to be a Christian.

Oh, to be sure, there are definitely some things you will have to give up. Christians are known for the things they stand for and the things they won't stand for. But you only give up those things that destroy you or cause pain and unhappiness. While you commit your life to Him without consideration

---

Man has been living subnormal for so long that he has come to believe that normal is abnormal.

---

of selfish pleasure, He responds by guiding you into the greatest life possible. A very important principle is found in 1 John 5:3: "This is the love of God, that we keep His commandments and His commandments are *not burdensome.*"

In the world today there are about two and one-half billion women. They come in assorted sizes, shapes, ages, colors and dispositions. Out of all those, God says that I am restricted to just one. I may choose whomever I please, as long as she is willing, but I may only choose one, and I must live faithful to her as long as we both live.

Why is that? Hasn't He unduly restricted me? Isn't He just trying to rob me of the joys the other women would bring?

No! It is for my benefit. He (the One who designed me) knows that this is the only way I am going to be fulfilled. His way makes me free—free to have the deep abiding joys that come only from a faithful Christian home. I am free to have the fulfillment and satisfaction for which everyone naturally yearns. I can think of nothing on earth more valuable than a genuine Christian home. And it is available only to those who honor His Word.

Why am I forbidden to get drunk? Same reasons. That way I am free to have a longer, healthier life, plus keep my family, my sanity, and my liver.

Christianity is what you were designed for. When your life follows the design of the Designer, it fits, and it feels good!!

The Balanced Life

A fulfilled life is one of holiness or wholeness. We have different kinds of needs. Those needs can be classified as physical, emotional, social, and spiritual. If I fill a part of these needs and not others, I will find some temporary thrills, but I will not be satisfied. I'll be incomplete.

There is a difference between a fulfilled life and temporary thrills. A man may be sitting in the middle of the street with a lampshade on his head and joyfully singing "Sweet Adeline" and yet be an unhappy, miserable person. Or a man can be undergoing a terrible pain or difficulty and be a secure, happy, fulfilled person.

The goal is to respond to *all* our basic needs. It's common, however, for people to neglect their spiritual needs. This causes widespread frustration and causes many to miss what they were designed to have.

People are designed to be different from animals. If the thrust of a person's life is to keep warm, keep his belly full, and remain sexually satisfied, then it's too bad he wasn't born a dog, or a horse, or a chicken. That's all *they* want. That's the way they were designed. Nothing more. Nothing deeper. Nothing higher.

You are different. The Bible says that you were created "in the image of God" (Genesis 1:26). You have a spiritual nature that has spiritual needs that you must not deny. In fact, you cannot deny them. It's not natural. It's not normal. It's going against your basic nature.

You can stop drinking water, but you can't keep from getting thirsty. You can stop eating, but you

---

Christianity is what you were designed for. When your life follows the design of the Designer, it fits, and it feels good!!

---

can't keep from getting hungry. You can stop relating to God, but you can't keep from yearning for God. It's the most normal and natural thing in the world.

Serving God doesn't make you strange. You yearn for God as easily and naturally as you yearn for water or food. But man has been living subnormal for so long that he has come to believe that normal is abnormal.

When you recognize and respond to your spiritual needs (which are natural and normal) along with your other needs, then your entire life takes on a new dimension, a new satisfaction.

It's the way you were designed!

Questions for Thought and Discussion

1. What unusual things do people do in order to appear normal?
2. Distinguish between a *normal* Christian life and an *average* Christian life.
3. Name some serendipities in your life. How is Matthew 6:33 life's greatest serendipity?
4. Why are there so many tense, unhappy religious fanatics?
5. What do you have to give up to be a Christian? Why does God require that?
6. What is the difference between a fulfilled life and a life filled with temporary thrills?
7. Why does man yearn so naturally for God?

CHAPTER 4

When Things Are Tough

Sometimes the statement "It depends on how you look at it" seems inadequate. Sometimes real, unfair, unreasonable tragedies occur. Children are born deformed or with fatal disorders. Loving, caring people have terrible accidents. We know that sometimes bad things happen to good people, and vice versa.

We would like to believe that we have complete control of our lives, and we can make everything work out right. But often things happen that are simply beyond our control. Sometimes they don't work out all right.

These situations do not negate the principle of controlling your life by choosing how to view things. In fact, times of tragedy are the most important times

---

Life isn't fair. It isn't supposed to be. Nobody said it was. All the energy we spend bewailing life's unfairness is wasted energy. When we get through, life's still unfair.

---

to apply this principle. Tragedies of one kind or another enter all our lives. Some people allow tragedy to overwhelm them. Others, with equal or greater loss, are able to work through tragedy and continue positive, victorious lives.

Even then, it depends on how you look at it.

Life Isn't Fair

Life isn't fair! It isn't supposed to be. Nobody said it was. All the energy we spend bewailing life's unfairness is wasted energy. When we get through, life's still unfair.

Jesus tells us clearly, "He causes His sun to rise on the evil and the good, and He sends the rain on the righteous and the unrighteous" (Matthew 5:45).

The Apostle Paul was a faithful, loving, tireless worker for the Lord. Yet, he was not supernaturally protected from tragedies. He lists imprisonments, beatings, stoning, shipwrecks, and all kinds of dangers and hardships that he had to bear (2 Corinthians 11:22-28).

Throughout history God's people have had to deal with real, unfair tragedies. It has always been that way. We must never be angry at God for failing to do what He never promised to do. He never promised a healthy, long life or that life would be fair. His promise is, "In the world you have tribulation, but take courage; I have overcome the world" (John 16:33).

An Example of How Not to Help

In the Old Testament, Job was suffering. He didn't understand it. He cried out in pain. He wanted to know why God was doing this to him. His friends, Eliphaz, Bildad, and Zophar misunderstood Job's utterance as a question of doubt rather than an exclamation of pain. Therefore, at the very time Job needed acceptance and reassurance the most, they gave him preaching and advice. Job didn't need scolding; he needed holding.

Today, when someone comes from the divorce court, hospital, or cemetery, they need a shoulder to cry on. They need someone to hear them as they express their pain, their helplessness, their confusion, and their despair. They don't need scolding; they need holding.

How Can I Help When Others Are Hurting?

When real difficulties come, well-meaning friends want to help. Sometimes their response is of great help, but sometimes it compounds the hurt.

Recently I had to stand by helplessly as my precious 22-year-old son, Danny, died. He was in the intensive care unit for almost a week, lingering between life and death. Many caring friends came by, each one sincerely wanting to help. Some helped, and some didn't. From that experience, let me share with you what did and what didn't help.

We were blessed by *brief* visits. This showed care and helped share the pain. When the visits were prolonged, they became a burden.

I didn't appreciate people asking for more details of Danny's condition than I offered. If I gave a general answer, it was because I *wanted* to give a general answer. I was made uncomfortable by those who pressed for more details.

Cards, flowers, and phone calls helped.

It was particularly helpful for visitors to offer to pray with us.

The one thing that not only didn't help but brought much pain was the visitors who wanted to talk about their friend or relative who had been in a coma, like Danny was. That *never* helped!

We were comforted when visitors shared their special memories of Danny. We enjoyed talking about him and remembering his bright, spicy personality. We still do.

Basically, we needed loving support. We didn't need advice. All those who later came to his funeral and sent cards were very helpful, even though we didn't get to speak to them personally.

In the months since his death, we had readjusted to life—life without him. It has been painful and difficult. It's supposed to be. Life has its painful times. But there has been a normal, healthy grief process, and we are doing very well.

Choose How to View It

The principle upon which this book is based has helped. If we chose to focus on how unfair it was for Danny to be born with his disorder, cystinosis, and to get to live only to 22, then we would have felt angry and cheated. But we recognize that none of us are promised another breath. Every moment of life is not to be expected but is a marvelous, unexpected blessing. Danny had over twenty-two years of that! What a blessing!

It depends on how we look at it.

Unhealthy Responses to Tragedies

There are some unhealthy ways to respond when tragedies come into our lives. Some responses impede the health process.

1. Misusing Hindsight

Some adults find it almost impossible to accept the fact that there are simply some things outside their control. They think they are supposed to be in charge. They cannot handle failure.

After a serious accident they punish themselves with the "if only's." "If only I'd started earlier (or later)." "If only I'd taken a different route." After a serious illness they say, "If only I had called the doctor sooner."

No one knows the future. We go along day by day making thousands of ordinary decisions. We only have the information before us at the time. Besides,

> *At the very time Job needed acceptance and reassurance the most, they gave him preaching and advice. Job didn't need scolding; he needed holding.*

if we *had* started earlier (or later), we have no way of knowing whether something worse might have happened. No one ever knows what would have happened if what happened hadn't happened.

2. Blaming Self

Those with the tendency to look backward tend to ask, "Where did I go wrong?" They blame themselves. This is especially true in cases where a child rebels or a mate leaves.

Of course, there are situations where they were so irresponsible that they drove the child or mate into rebellion. If this is true, they need to make appropriate corrections in their lives. However, they might have done nothing wrong. Often we punish ourselves unnecessarily.

We all know of good, godly parents who poured their lives into their children and had one or more of them go wrong. There's the mother who discovers her beloved teenage daughter is pregnant. There is the loving, Christian dad who is called to the police station where his son has been arrested for possessing drugs. Where did they go wrong? Maybe nowhere.

Ours is the first generation to blame the parents when children rebel. Previously they blamed the child. "Your parents didn't bring you up that way!" It may well be that the child was given the right direction and willingly chose to go against the grain.

God had two special children, Adam and Eve. How did they turn out? They rebelled, didn't they? Was that God's fault? Was He to blame? No. They chose, on their own, to go contrary to what they were taught. They alone were to blame. If this is true of God, how about cutting *yourself* some slack?

Proverbs 22:6 states, "Train up a child in the way he should go, and when he is old he will not depart from it." This verse has been preached as though it was a promise of God. This has caused many broken-hearted parents to feel unnecessary pangs of guilt.

Proverbs are proverbs. They are not promises. A proverb is a statement of *general* truth, but there can be exceptions.

Notice Proverbs 13:4: "The sluggard craves and gets nothing." Is that a promise of God? No, its a proverb. It is generally (but not always) true. Most sluggards get very little, but occasionally one does all right.

It is generally true that if you train up a child in the way he should go that when he is old he will not depart from it. But that's not a promise. He still has free will. He still must choose for himself.

If there were something we could do to win back every wayward child or to insure their faithfulness, there would never be a broken-hearted Christian parent. Romans 14:12 says, "Each one of us shall give account of *himself* to God." Everyone is ultimately responsible for his *own* behavior.

Self recrimination is an unhealthy way of responding to tragedy. "Poor me, I'm just no good" is an attitude that leads to depression and withdrawal. It doesn't help.

3. *Blame Others*

Another common mistake is to blame others. Instead of channeling energy toward solutions and healings, some people are caught up in finding someone or something to blame. This, too, is counterproductive.

4. *Misusing Anger*

Another unhealthy way of responding to tragedy is to strike out in anger. It's like the person who stubs his toe on the chair leg, then kicks the chair. Or, he can't loosen the nut, so he throws the wrench.

At the time of tragedy, such as death in the family, everyone should be careful about how he responds to others. Emotions are high. It is not uncommon for things to be said or done without thinking that cause pain in relationships for years.

Summary

Change whatever you need to change. Accept what you cannot change. Repent, if necessary. Receive forgiveness, and go on. The Apostle Paul had enough sins in his past to drive him crazy, had he focused on them and dwelt on them. However, he received forgiveness and put them behind him. He said, "This one thing I do: forgetting what lies behind, and reaching forward to what lies ahead, I press on . . ." (Philippians 3:13).

Another unhealthy way of responding to tragedy is to strike out in anger. It's like the person who stubs his toe on the chair leg, then kicks the chair. Or, he can't loosen the nut, so he throws the wrench.

Some things are simply beyond our control. It is quite impossible to live an entire life without having to deal with some tough times, some tragedies. By choosing how to view them, you can deal with them victoriously.

In *all* situations praise God and give Him glory. This is our purpose on earth.

Questions for Thought and Discussion

1. Do you agree that life isn't fair? Give examples.
2. Why do we think that life is supposed to be fair?
3. Do you know anyone who has blamed God for failing to do something He never promised to do?
4. Have you had a time of tragedy in your life? How well have you dealt with it?
5. What things do friends do that help in time of difficulty? What things fail to help? Give examples.
6. Name some unhealthy or ineffective ways of trying to deal with tragedy. Can you give examples?
7. Are parents always to blame when a child rebels? Is a husband or wife always to blame when a mate leaves? Explain.
8. How can the principle of choosing how to view things help during times of real tragedy?

CHAPTER 5

The Power of a Dream

It was a hot, sultry, humid day. The young stranger and his friends had been walking for several hours. Now he sat down by a well while his friends went to find a place to buy some food.

A solitary figure, a woman carrying a waterpot, approached. Her sandaled feet scuffed little puffs of dust about her ankles as she walked.

At first neither of them spoke, but they were very much aware of the other's presence. The young stranger broke the silence. "Give me a drink," he said. The conversation that followed radically changed the life and the lifestyle of that woman.

Afterward, she was so excited that she ran back to her village, forgetting her waterpot and leaving it behind. She shared the news of what she had heard. A whole group started out to see this young stranger—Jesus.

When they were still a distance away, He and His friends could see them and hear their excited voices. Jesus said to His disciples, "Lift up your eyes, and look on the fields, that they are white for the harvest" (John 4:35).

He was correcting their vision. He wanted them to look beyond the surface—to get a dream. He wanted them to see what could happen, and He knew that so much depended on how they looked at it.

Success Begins with a Dream

The first essential step in any worthwhile endeavor is to visualize. You must see the results in your mind before you begin. Success begins with a dream.

The bleakest point in Israel's history in the Old Testament was the destruction of Jerusalem by the Babylonians. King Nebuchadnezzar led the siege, and the beautiful, holy city was razed. The magnificent temple and the stately walls were destroyed, and the inhabitants were carried away into slavery.

Generations later the Jews were allowed to return. For over eighty years after their return they lived there with no movement toward rebuilding the walls. The walls continued to lay in ruins.

Then Nehemiah came along. He had a dream. He went to Jerusalem and viewed the situation. The Jews had for years seen only ruined walls. They probably stepped over the rubble in their daily activities. Nehemiah saw, in his mind, the rebuilt walls. The Old Testament book of Nehemiah is the story of the valiant rebuilding of the walls against incredible odds. All this began because one man dared to dream.

Five Steps to Success

You can't get started in any worthwhile endeavor without a dream. In fact, it is the essential first step in the five-step process that leads to success. The process is to visualize, organize, deputize, supervise, and analyze.

1. *First, visualize.* This is the dream. Get a clear picture in your mind of what success will look like. Know where you are going.

2. *Second, organize.* Chart a course that will lead you from where you are to your dream. Develop a strategy that will lead you to your goal. When this is done properly, it brings a feeling of satisfaction and confidence. You can be satisfied with not being at your destination, as long as you know that you are on your way.

3. *Third, deputize.* Recruit any others needed to help you reach your goal. This is the process of delegation.

4. *Fourth, supervise.* Make sure that all the elements of the strategy you developed are proceeding properly. You may have to make adjustments as needed.

5. *Fifth, analyze.* After you have reached (or missed) your goal, it is good to look over the process for your own enlightenment.

There Is Power in A Dream

Until recently, I planted a large vegetable garden each spring. It was a lot of work—plowing, digging, making furrows, planting. But it was a joy. When I dropped those seeds into the ground, I didn't see

---

The first essential step in any worthwhile endeavor is to visualize. You must see the results in your mind before you begin. Success begins with a dream.

---

seeds—I saw tomatoes, and squash, and okra, and corn. I saw them as mature, healthy, and delicious! That delightful image in my mind motivated me not only to do the work, but to enjoy it immensely. There is power inherent within a dream.

Some young people do well in college, and others do poorly. More important than their I.Q. is their dream.

My oldest son, Jeff, is very bright. Yet, when he attended Abilene Christian University, he almost flunked out. Later, after he was married and had worked for awhile at entry-level jobs, he returned to college. This time he was easily at the top of his classes. What changed? His dreams changed. Now he is well on his way to a productive and successful career.

Mel Weldon does much counseling with people in the bay area of California where he lives. One of his techniques is to ask a discouraged person to tell him what he would *like* to be like. When he does, Mel turns and types that on to a prescription pad. He than hands the "prescription" to the person with the instructions to read it three times a day for a month. Mel is aware that, if you keep a dream before you, it will be internalized into your subconscious.

Marcus Aurelius said, "A man's life is what his thoughts make of it." Ralph Waldo Emerson wrote, "A man *is* what he thinks about all day long." What goes into our minds comes out in our actions. Our entire direction of life depends on where we choose to focus. It is within our control.

The monumental text from the Bible that states this principle is from Paul's writings: "But we all, with unveiled face beholding as in a mirror the glory of the Lord, are being transformed into the same image . . ." (2 Corinthians 3:18).

The power inherent in a dream is both positive and negative. We will be transformed into *any image* we keep before us. That's why pornography and cheap, dirty TV is so bad, and why good positive dreams are so vital.

A Desire Is Required

To bring the dream into reality, we must desire it. "I've got to do it!" Desire is a part of the dream that has power.

Just because something is unquestionably best for us does not necessarily mean that we have sufficient desire to bring it about. Jesus once asked an unusual question. He came across a man who had been sick for thirty-eight years. One would normally *assume* that he wanted to get well. But Jesus asked the sick man, "Do you want to get well?" (John 5:6). The sick man's desire was important.

Once there was a man walking through a graveyard late at night. He was somewhat uneasy and trying to be brave. He didn't see the freshly dug grave and stumbled into it. Frantic, he began clawing at the dirt sides but was unable to get out. He regained control and thought, "I will just sit here quietly, and when they come to use the grave tomorrow they can lift me out."

However, another man, more skittish than he, came along and stumbled into the same grave. Not knowing that there was anyone else there, he began clawing at the sides. Suddenly he heard the man in the corner say, "You can't get out of here." But he *did*! There's power in real desire!

A hunter was being chased by an angry bear. The bear was getting closer and closer. There was only one tree, and the lowest branch was twenty feet up. The hunter knew it was his only chance; so, he jumped with all his might. But alas, he missed it.

However, he caught it on the way *down!* There's power in real desire.

Why are some people able to keep on a regular exercise program and others are not? It's the difference in desire. Some people not only *see* the need more clearly but also *want* the results more intensely.

Susan knew clearly that she should quit smoking. She was a registered nurse and was aware of the

---

The power inherent in a dream is both positive and negative. We will be transformed into any image we keep before us. That's why pornography and cheap, dirty TV is so bad, and why good positive dreams are so vital.

---

medical information linking smoking and all kinds of illnesses. She tried several times but was unable to quit. She was unable, that is, until one day when her doctor detected some precancerous cell tissue in her lungs. Suddenly, she was able to quit easily. In fact, you couldn't force her to take a cigarette! What made the difference? Desire.

The Bible says, "Delight yourself in the Lord, and He will *give* you the *desires* of your heart" (Psalms 37:4).

Be Willing to Dare

Plan with faith! Dream with courage! Plan big! Why can't you be the very best? Why can't you have the very best?

The Apostle Paul had the right spirit. He said, "I

can do *all things* through Christ who strengthens me" (Philippians 4:13).

We must not dream and plan based only on the past. If we do, we will never grow beyond it. Remember, until something changes, everything stays the same. We must dare to dream big dreams and then to act on them.

An unknown insightful author wrote the following lines:

> Little and great is man.
> Great if he will
> Or, if he will, a pygmy still
> For what he will, he can.

Summary

You cannot grow bigger than your dreams. Don't be afraid to dream big dreams and keep them before you.

I don't know where you're going with your life, but I do know the first step—"lift up your eyes." Dream a great dream! It depends on how you look at it.

Questions for Thought and Discussion

1. List and discuss the five-step process that leads to success.
2. How does one's dream affect his success or failure in college?
3. Give examples of power inherent in a dream.
4. Give both positive and negative examples of the principle, "You actualize what you visualize."
5. Is it true that you know that something is best for you and, yet, have insufficient desire to bring it about? Give examples.
6. Why must our dreams and plans not be based solely on the past?
7. Look at your life. What could you do if you really dared to dream big dreams?

MY LIFE
WITH
OTHERS

CHAPTER 6

Making Your Marriage Sparkle

God is so wise! It's hard to imagine a being so wise as to come up with the idea of male and female. He designed each sex to be special. He placed in each one the qualities especially desired and needed by the other.

After 32 years of marriage, I still sometimes look at Martha and am almost overcome with pure delight. It has been that way from the first. Each stage of our life together has been better than all the others.

When we were first married, what joy we found in having and loving each other! It seemed that nothing could ever be better than that.

Then the babies came along. How precious! How delightful! We loved them so much. It was almost unreal.

As they grew into their own personalities and developed their own values and faith, we were so proud. They were so much fun. Certainly *this* was the best time of life.

Then they became adults. Jeff, Stacey and Roger all married within a three-year period. We happily welcomed their mates as our new son and daughters. How fulfilled we felt.

Now there are just the two of us again. We can focus our attention completely on each other again.

We also find so much pleasure when our grandchildren visit; they are so delightful. I think, again, that surely it just can't get any better than this.

Of course, we also had our struggles along the way. That's all right; we expected them.

Available to Everyone

I'm aware that everyone doesn't find the fulfillment in marriage that they desire. In my counseling practice I see them all the time. But it is *available* to everyone. There is a way to make your marriage sparkle with all the joy and fulfillment that God intended when He designed you as He did. In other words, God has given us laws and principles, and when these are followed, marriage works. When they are ignored, it doesn't work.

I tend to agree with the counselor who said, "There are no incompatible couples; there are only unwilling individuals."

In fact, there are many cultures where the marriage is arranged by parents. The couple has nothing to say about it. They meet on their wedding day. Those cultures tend to do much better than ours in producing lasting and satisfying marriages.

I am not recommending that arrangement for selecting a mate, but I am recommending that attitude toward marriage. It is permanent. There are no alternatives. Both individuals must be willing to work it out.

The Meaning of Love

Our culture particularly stresses the importance of love in a healthy relationship. Our culture is right. Love is important. However, Hollywood has given us a wrong definition of love. In fact, it's often unclear what we mean by the word.

I said, "I love spaghetti," and I say, "I love Martha." I get two entirely different feelings when I look at a plate of spaghetti and when I look at Martha. They are both pleasant, but very different. Yet, I describe them both by the word "love."

The Greeks have four different words with four different meanings that we translate with one English word as "love."

First is *agapao*. The important thing about this word is that it does not describe a feeling. It is a *decision* to put another's needs ahead of your own. God commands me to love *(agapao)* my wife. He also commands me to love *(agapao)* my enemies. He is not commanding me to *feel* toward my enemies as I feel toward my wife. He is commanding me to put them ahead of myself (see Romans 12:20).

"God so loved *(agapao)* the world that He gave His only begotten Son" (John 3:16). That does not mean that He enjoyed, or felt good about, allowing His Son to be crucified. No, it means He put our needs ahead of His own.

Second is *Phileo*. Basically, this *is* describing a feeling. This is what a seventeen-year-old boy means when he looks into his girlfriend's eyes and says, "Do you love me?" But it's not just boy-girl. It has nothing to do with sexuality. I love *(phileo)* Ernie Gill. He and I were missionaries together for years. He is a dear friend. I feel good when we are together.

Third is *Eros*, from which we get the word "erotic." This is the word for sexual attraction.

Fourth is *Storgé*. It means family attraction. If my mother were not my mother, I would think she was a very nice lady, but because she is my mother, my feelings toward her are very different. I have special feelings for brothers, sisters, cousins, etc.

Our Limited View

In our culture, when we think or speak of love, we ordinarily mean *phileo* or *eros*. We think of the feelings or of the sexual attraction. The problem comes when we try to build a life or a marriage on those two. There are two reasons why it won't work.

The first reason is because these two fluctuate. The second reason is that we have little or no control

> *The counterpart of "wives submit to your husband" is not "husbands command your wives." It is "husbands love your wives." He is to be her lover, not her commander.*

over their fluctuation. Feelings are not subject to our immediate control. We all have mood swings. Sometimes I want Martha sitting on my lap, but some other times I want her to leave me alone and let me watch the football game.

The point is, if we try to build any relationship, especially marriage, on those two definitions of love alone, it will be short-lived. It cannot survive.

I recall a scene from my favorite musical, *Fiddler on the Roof*. Tevye had been surprised that one of his daughters wanted to choose her own husband based on their feelings for each other, rather than marrying the man he would choose for her. As he thought of his own marriage, he turned to his wife, Golda, and sang, "Do you love me?" She answered, "I bore your children." He said, "I know," then sang, "but do you love me?" She said, "I cook your food." He again sang, "But do you love me?" Until then they knew their marriage was based on love *(agapao)* because they served each other. Now he wanted to know if she also loved *(phileo)* him.

You can build a marriage, and a life, on *agapao*. You cannot build any lasting relationship on *phileo* or *eros*. The only understanding of love that is within your control is *agapao*. You can *always choose* to put your family's needs ahead of your own—no matter how you happen to be feeling.

It depends on how you look at it.

God's Description of the Roles of Husband and Wife

Christians learn their theology from the Bible, not from the culture around them. The role of husband and wife in a Christian marriage in described in the Bible. It is constant. It is often a variance with the shifting concepts in our changing culture. These roles are described in Ephesians 5:22-23.

"Wives, be subject to your own husbands, as to the Lord. For the husband is the head of the wife, as Christ also is the head of the church, He Himself being the Savior of the body. But as the church is subject to Christ, so also the wives ought to be to their husbands in everything.

"Husbands, love your wives, just as Christ also loved the church and gave Himself up for her; that He might sanctify her, having cleansed her by the washing of water with the word, that He might present to Himself the church in all her glory, having no spot or wrinkle or any such thing; but that she should be holy and blameless. So husbands ought also to love their own wives as their own bodies. He who loves his own wife loves himself; for no one ever hated his own flesh, but nourishes and cherishes it, just as Christ also does the church, because we are members of His body. For this cause a man shall leave his father and mother, and shall cleave to his wife; and the two shall become one flesh. This mystery is great; but I am speaking with reference to Christ and the church. Nevertheless let each individual among you also love his own wife even as himself; and let the wife see to it that she respect her husband."

The Christian Wife

First, the wife's role. "Wives, be subject to your own husbands, as to the Lord. For the husband is the head of the wife as Christ also is the head of the church."

The word describing her role is to be "subject" or to be "submissive." I am well aware that this is contrary to our modern cultural teaching, but our theology comes from the Bible.

Man and woman are equal before God. In fact, Galatians 3:28 tells us that as far as equality is concerned, "there is neither Jew nor Greek, bond nor free, *male* nor *female*." While man and woman are equal in their relationship with God, husbands and wives do not have the same functions within the marriage.

One is no more important than the other. Which is more important, a lock or a key? Neither one. Together they form a functioning unit. Each plays its own unique role. The same is true with husband and wife.

The wife is to respect her husband's position in the home, not because he is the biggest, the fastest, or the loudest. And, certainly not because he is the smartest (for often he isn't). She respects his position because God put him there, and her respect is constant. Her role is not based on how well she thinks he is doing with his role. It is based on God's constant command and design in her life.

What if her husband is not a Christian? Should she still be submissive to him? The answer is yes. He is still her husband. Specific instructions for such a case are given in 1 Peter 3:1-4. It tells of how he may be won to Christ by her gentle spirit.

When I first met Diana Venegoni, she was eager to hear the gospel. She responded to it beautifully, and she began to grow in Christ. I had never met her husband, John, because he didn't attend church with her, but everytime she spoke of him it was with obvious love and respect. She seemed to glow at the mention of him. Then John began attending church services, too. He was somewhat skeptical at first. Diana continued to be faithful to Christ and lovingly responsive to John. Soon, he gave his life to Christ. They are now an example of a caring Christian family.

The Christian Husband

We now turn to the husband's role in the marriage, and we begin to see the balance and fairness. The Ephesians passage tells him to "love your wife." And it tells how much—"as Christ loved the church," and "as your own body."

The counterpart of "wives submit to your husband" is *not* "husbands *command* your wives." It is "husbands *love* your wives." He is to be her lover, not her commander.

The Greek word for love here is *agapao*—the most unselfish kind of love. It's love that seeks only her good, the kind of love Christ has for the church.

He desires to please her. His love is tender, and responsive, and gentle. He does nothing to bring her any pain or hurt. Her happiness and welfare is dearer to him than his own. He recognizes that she is every bit as adult, bright and capable as he is. He responds to her as a "joint-heir" with him (1 Peter 3:7). He is aware that when she willingly submits to his leadership it makes her very vulnerable. He must never take advantage of that vulnerability any more than Christ would take advantage of the church.

Getting What You Invite

Having seen the roles of husbands and wives, we now note that each should help the other fulfill his/her role. He can make it very difficult for her to respect him and then condemn her for not doing it. She can be very unlovable and wonder why he isn't as tender as he should be. Or both can make it easy for the other. It all depends on them. We usually get what we invite, seldom what we demand.

Broad Enough to Allow Variety

The roles of husband and wife are not narrow and restrictive. There is plenty of room for each relationship to be uniquely fashioned to meet the needs of each couple.

The relationship between Martha and me is very dependent. We depend heavily on each other. If I'm going to be gone for a couple of days, we plan for it for a week. It's a big deal. We love our relationship, and I thought that everyone ought to have one just like ours.

Our friends, Ira and June Hill, have a very independent relationship—quite different from ours. He flies all around the country and the world in his business. He comes and goes all the time. They can be quite independent. They love it. It fits them.

If you want to know a sure-fire way of improving your marriage, ignore the behavior you want to have decreased. Lovingly reinforce the behavior you want to have increased.

Seeing a very different, but equally satisfying, relationship helped me to understand the tremendous varieties available within the Christian roles. I have often used them as examples of this variety. The last time we were with the Hills we had a good laugh. He had noticed the same thing and had used *us* as an example of the same thing in his teaching.

The One Main Task

Every married person has this one primary task—to discover the needs of his/her partner and cheerfully meet them. As long as you keep doing that, life will keep getting better.

Dr. Paul Faulkner, Chairman of the Family Studies Department of Abilene Christian University, tells this story:

It seems a lady told her counselor that she could not stand her terrible husband. She not only wanted to leave him, but she wanted to do so in such a way as to bring him the most possible pain.

The counselor explained that if she left him now, since she had been so hateful to him, he would probably be happy about it.

So, he advised her to spend six months warmly serving him, caring for his needs, making him feel strong and manly. Then, when she left, he would really hurt. She agreed to do it.

After seven months the counselor saw her again and asked how it went when she left. She replied, "Oh, my husband has become the warmest, lovingest, caringest man on earth. I wouldn't think of leaving him."

The one single factor that is characteristic of a functional, healthy, happy home is that both husband and wife focus on meeting the needs of the other.

If you want to know a sure-fire way of improving your marriage, do this for one month—no, for three months: stop trying to change your mate. Accept the warts and all. Ignore the behavior you want to have decreased. Lovingly reinforce the behavior you want to have increased. Every day help him/her feel good, and important, and *very* special.

I guarantee it will work!

Questions for Thought and Discussion

1. What stage of life have you found to be most delightful?
2. Do you agree with the counselor who said, "There are no incompatible couples; there are only unwilling individuals"? Explain.
3. Why do you think the divorce rate has risen so dramatically in the last 50 years?
4. Distinguish between the four Greek words which are translated into the one English word "love."
5. How does a limited view of love cause a breakdown of marriages?
6. Describe the biblical role of the Christian wife.
7. Describe the biblical role of the Christian husband.
8. When is it most difficult for either mate to live up to his or her role?
9. What one thing does the author say you can do to improve your marriage? How, specifically, would you go about doing that?

CHAPTER 7

What About Me, I'm Single?

There are all kinds of single people. Some are old, some are young. There are the divorced, widowed, and never married. Some are single by choice, others by circumstances.

One single lady recently assured me that she could marry any man she *pleased*. Then she wistfully added, "But I seldom *please* any of them."

Some are leading radiant, victorious lives of service. Some are not. There are ways to view and approach single life that lead to victory, and there are ways that lead to defeat. It depends on how you look at it.

The number of singles in our society is growing larger. Several factors contribute to this—the high divorce rate, a tendency to delay marriage, more people choosing not to marry and, as people live longer, an extended period of widowhood.

The church where I am a member is average in its make-up. One out of six adults is single. In a nearby congregation, of the last 100 new adult members, forty-six were single. Unfortunately, the church is not responding adequately to this large, growing segment of our society.

Singleness Has Advantages

Singleness, like everything else, has some advantages and some disadvantages. Both are real. The ones on which an individual chooses to focus will determine the direction of his life.

Remember, Jesus was single. The Apostle Paul was single. He focused on the advantages of being single and changed the world for Christ.

As he wrote a letter to his friends in Corinth he listed three benefits of being single. They are found in 1 Corinthians 7:25-35. His main point is that for some Christians the single life, at least for a time, is best, but it's not demanded.

Singleness Is Honorable

It is particularly admirable for a person to choose not to enter into marriage in order to devote himself, or herself, more fully to study, prayer, being conformed to His image, and to ministry. This may be for a limited time or for a lifetime.

Accordingly, it is ironic that we often give a kind of second-class status to singles when the Bible gives them special honor. Notice how many sermons, classes, programs and workshops we have that are to help people make the most of their marriage. Notice, too, how few we have to help people make the most of their singleness.

I am not *downgrading* marriage. It came from God. I love Christian weddings. I am very grateful for my own marriage. I am *upgrading* the place singles are generally given. It is particularly honorable.

Some authors say that if you are unmarried you are incomplete. There is a technical, theological word for that—baloney! That concept is contrary to scriptures.

The Present Distress

The first benefit Paul lists for singleness is "in view of the present distress" (1 Corinthians 7:26). It must be noted that the specific distress to which he was referring does not apply to most of us in our culture. He had reference to the persecution that had begun, first by the Jews and then by the Romans.

It's not hard to see how singleness would have been a definite advantage when the persecution was intense: more flexibility, not having the care of a mate or of children, avoiding the possibility of witnessing *their* torture.

There are universal principles that always apply but find different expressions in different cultures. For example, the universal principle of humility and service was expressed in New Testament times by washing another's feet. We express it in other ways.

The principle here is that a Christian will forego *any* pleasure that keeps him from being the best possible servant of God. When they applied it in their "present distress," it called for some of them to remain single.

To apply that principle in your life, answer this question: What is there in your life that you know you have the "right" to do, but you also know that you would be a better servant or example if you didn't? Whatever that is, remember our purpose in life is to honor God, not find pleasure or exercise our "rights."

Some Christians, when applying this principle, will decide to remain single, at least for a time. Praise God for them!

Less Worldly Concern

A second benefit of being single Paul states in verse 28. It is actually a disadvantage of being married. "Yet such will have trouble in this life." Another translation reads, "will have worldly concern."

Some singles think that nothing could be worse than being single for the rest of their life. Wrong. There is one thing worse—being married to the wrong person for the rest of their life.

For every single who comes to my counseling center struggling with his or her singleness, I have at least twenty who come struggling with their marriage. Marriage, too, has both advantages and disadvantages.

What "worldly concerns" was Paul suggesting would be avoided by remaining single? There are constant

---

It is ironic that we often give a kind of second-class status to singles when the Bible gives them special honor.

---

adjustments. His basic nature, his flaws, and his moods must fit in with her basic nature, her flaws, and her moods. They must merge all this with the nature, flaws and moods of their children. All this takes energy and time.

Bill Cosby says that you don't qualify as a parent if you just have one child because, if something is broken or messed up, you know who did it.

It's true that the greatest joys of my life have come from my family. It is also true that the most intense pain in my life has come from my family. Every family has its share of "worldly concerns."

These concerns are significantly magnified when a Christian chooses to marry a non-Christian.

More Time Available for Ministry

The third benefit of being single, which Paul lists in verses 29 to 31, is that more *time* is available. Singles (except single parents) do not have the same claims on their lives as those with families. They have more flexibility. This can be a marvelous opportunity for growth and for ministry.

Family time can be rich time, good time, and important time, but it is time that must be reserved by marrieds that is available to singles for other uses. That time can be a tremendous benefit if used wisely.

Some of God's greatest servants were singles who used the flexibility of their time to honor God. The Apostle Paul stated that he had the "right to take along a believing wife, even as the rest of the apostles" (1 Corinthians 9:5). He chose not to, and the flexibility this allowed him was used wisely, and God was honored.

Among my acquaintances I think of Landon Saunders, who devotes his entire life to the *Heartbeat* program. Big Don Williams from Pepperdine University serves young people all over the country. Mary Lou Rodriquez spends three weeks per month helping in an orphanage in Mexico. Many others serve in ministries more effectively because they are single.

Dealing with Loneliness

Loneliness can be very real. It can rob us of physical, emotional and spiritual energy. When we are in its grip it seems never-ending, as if it will go on forever. C. S. Lewis described it as "stretching away like a desert." King David described it this way in Psalm 88:4-8, 18: "I am counted among those who go down to the pit; I am like a man without strength.

I am set apart with the dead, like the slain who lie in the grave, whom you remember no more, who are cut off from your care. You have put me in the lowest pit, in the darkest depths. Your wrath lies heavily upon me; you have overwhelmed me with all your waves. You have taken from me my closest friends and have made me repulsive to them. I am confined and cannot escape; You have taken my companions and loved ones from me; the darkness is my closest friend."

Time alone does not necessarily cause loneliness. It can, but there is a significant difference between being alone and being lonely. It depends on how you look at it.

Unhealthy Ways to Deal with Loneliness

A common mistake singles make is to simply sit alone and hurt. This allows loneliness to feed on itself, and it only gets worse. This sets up a loneliness cycle. I feel lonely; so I begin thinking lonely thoughts, which leads to acting in lonely ways, which makes me feel even lonelier, and on and on.

Another common mistake is to get involved in unchristian activities, such as singles bars or unchristian groups. This, too, usually makes things worse.

Some authors say that if you are unmarried you are incomplete. There is a technical, theological word for that—baloney! That concept is contrary to scripture.

Almost all relationships there are shallow, short-lived, and painful. No one can live outside the will of God and succeed.

In order to make these relationships work, we must *pretend* that attention means respect, pleasant encounters mean a fulfilled life, brief intimacy means caring, and sex means love.

Unfortunately, we soon discover that those experiences don't satisfy but only reawaken and underscore the feeling of real loneliness along with a heavy load of guilt.

"Do not be deceived, God is not mocked; for whatever a man sows, this will he also reap" (Galatians 6:7). God's way is always best.

Healthy Ways to Deal with Time Alone

We can break the loneliness cycle by *choosing* to involve ourselves in some activity with others, even though we may not *feel* like it. One of the most helpful concepts that O. H. Mowrer teaches is, "It is easier to act yourself into a better way of feeling than to feel yourself into a better way of acting." That is such a powerful principle!

The direction of your life is in your hands. You can turn yourself outward and grow, or you can turn yourself inward and wither. You must lose yourself in service and ministry. Find something worth giving your life to, and go for it.

My Dad died in 1984. He and my mother had been very close during their 59 years of marriage. After his death Mom felt a lot of loneliness. She had to adjust to being alone and pour her life into serving others before it got better. She's done a marvelous job. She turned 80 last June, and she's still serving others. She's a great example.

Your attitude, not your singleness, causes loneliness. Therefore, getting married isn't always the solution. Some of the most lonely people I know are married. John Denver has a song entitled "Seasons of the Heart." It tells of two married partners together

> *Some singles think that nothing could be worse than being single for the rest of their life. Wrong. There is one thing worse—being married to the wrong person for the rest of their life.*

for years. Then comes the tragic line, "when I am lying right beside you is when I feel the most alone of all."

Singleness brings the need for creative thinking and prayer to deal with loneliness. It also brings the significant benefit of more flexible time.

God's Best

You who are single need not wonder why you have missed God's best. You *have* God's best. You *are* God's best! At least for now it is God's call for you to be single. There are unique advantages to that. Find them in your situation. Use them to His glory.

It depends on how you look at it.

Questions for Thought and Discussion

1. What could the church do to respond more adequately to the growing number of singles in our community?
2. Name some ways we overlook or give a second-class status to singles.
3. What did Paul mean that singleness was preferable "in view of the present distress"? How does that relate to our culture?
4. How do singles have "less worldly concern"? When might they have *more* worldly concern?
5. How do singles have more time available for ministry? When might they have *less* time available for ministry?
6. Name some unhealthy ways to deal with loneliness.
7. Name some singles you know who have creatively used their singleness to serve others.
8. What is the difference between being *alone* and being *lonely*? Explain.

CHAPTER 8

Does It Work for Teens, Too?

What about teenagers? Does it depend on how they look at it, too? You bet it does! And the sooner they grasp this powerful principle, the more successful their lives will be.

Jesus tells the world's most famous short story in Luke, chapter 15. We often call it the parable of the prodigal son. One could not find a clearer illustration of the principle we are exploring in this book. Whether this young man's life was to be a fulfilled one at home or an empty one in a pig pen depended on how he chose to view things.

Here's the story from Luke 15:11-24.

"There was a man who had two sons. The younger one said to his father, 'Father, give me my share of the estate.' So he divided his property between them.

"Not long after that, the younger son got together all he had, set off for a distant country and there squandered his wealth in wild living. After he had spent everything, there was a severe famine in that whole country, and he began to be in need. So he went and hired himself out to a citizen of that country, who sent him to his fields to feed pigs. He longed to fill his stomach with the pods that the pigs were eating, but no one gave him anything.

"When he came to his senses, he said, 'How many of my father's hired men have food to spare, and here I am starving to death! I will set out and go back to my father and say to him: "Father, I have sinned against heaven and against you. I am no longer worthy to be called your son; make me like one of your hired men."' So he got up and went to his father.

"But while he was still a long way off, his father saw him and was filled with compassion for him; he ran to his son, threw his arms around him and kissed him.

"The son said to him, 'Father, I have sinned against heaven and against you. I am no longer worthy to be called your son.'

"But the father said to his servants, 'Quick! Bring the best robe and put it on him. Put a ring on his finger and sandals on his feet. Bring the fattened calf and kill it. Let's have a feast and celebrate. For this son of mine was dead and is alive again; he was lost and is found.' So they began to celebrate."

The main lesson is God's concern for each individual and his willingness to forgive. But it is also a story of teen rebellion.

Every teenager has a normal, healthy need to develop independence. The apron strings must be cut. During childhood, parents were looked to as the ultimate source of wisdom. "My Daddy said so" was an appeal to the highest authority.

During adolescence this changes. The statement becomes "that's *your* opinion." Teens must question authority as they develop independence based on their own world view and values. This inevitable process always brings some conflict. In healthy families this can usually be worked through and the stress kept to a minimum.

Sometimes, however, teens rebel. Like the young man in Jesus' story, they go into a "distant country." Fortunately, some find their way back. In fact, there are many of us who can look back on an ugly period in our lives. We went into the distant country and made it back, but it's a particularly perilous and risky journey. Most people who go into the distant country never make it back.

Many Die in the Distant Country

We have no promise of another day. We have all been to funerals of young people. Death is not reserved just for the elderly.

Kelly McCain was a beautiful, bright, healthy Christian girl. Everyone loved her. We all expected her to grow up into a fine Christian lady. The future seemed filled with promise. A few days before her thirteenth birthday she caught the flu. No big deal,

You can't unscramble eggs—or lives. Sin, that we thought would be a delightful servant, becomes our master.

we thought. On her birthday she entered the hospital and lost consciousness. A few days later she died of an unusual complication called Reyes Syndrome.

We all, like Kelly, are subject to our own mortality. "Life is like a vapor that appears for a little while and then (often without warning) vanishes away." Therefore we all, like Kelly, should remain in our Father's house. Even a brief trip to the distant country is far too risky.

Many Do Not Come to Their Senses

The story Jesus told has a turning point. It has a happy ending. The young man, sitting among the pigs, discovered the logical result of viewing life as he did. He changed the way he looked at it. That changed his life. In the story it says, "he came to his senses."

Sometimes that happens, but not always. Not even usually. People usually continue in the direction they are headed.

Think of all the people who were brought up in good, Christian homes who have walked away. They usually expected it to be a brief journey, but they are still there. Most do not return.

I have a brother, Wayne, who is two years older than I. We grew up together. We had the same loving Christian parents. We shared the same room.

When Wayne was a teenager, he rebelled against his spiritual training and went into the distant country. He didn't expect to stay. I know. I was there. He expected to "live it up" for a little while and then return.

Wayne turned 57 last August. At that time he was still in the distant country. He had married a remarkable Christian lady. He had been blessed with three children. They had grown up, married and established their own homes. And Wayne was still in the distant country. What he expected to be a brief trip had lasted for decades—the major part of his life.

Unlike the norm, this story has a happy ending. A few months ago Wayne came home from the distant country. He committed his life to Christ and was born again. While we rejoice with his return, it also underscores how unusual it is to change at his stage of life. Most never "come to their senses."

It Depends on How You Look at It

How many people do you think are now saying to themselves, "I know I'm not living right, and *later* I'm going to change and do better?" How many? Thousands? Millions? How many of those do you think will ever get around to it? A few. Very, very few. Most people who go into the distant country never return.

Many Come To Themselves Too Late

It must be made clear that it is never too late to receive God's forgiveness. That is always available. No matter who the person or what the sin, God stands ready to run to him and welcome him home. That's the main point of this story. That's the nature of God.

While we can always be released from the guilt of sin, we still must deal with its consequences. Many people come to their senses in the distant country only to find that they have formed permanent or unalterable situations that cannot be reversed. Even after receiving the Father's forgiveness, they must deal with the consequences for a lifetime.

Some have messed their lives up with drugs. This obviously includes the many thousands who are addicted. Even after receiving forgiveness, they are still addicted. It must still be dealt with and it will be tough.

Randy came to see me at the counseling center. He was 26 years old. He had the appearance of one who had lived a rough life. He had been involved with paint sniffing for quite a while. He *now* saw what a mistake it was. He was genuinely sorry, and he truly repented. He wished he had never done it. He, like the boy in the story, "came to his senses."

Unfortunately, he had destroyed so many brain cells that he could now barely function outside an institution. He was incapable of gainful employment and would never be normal again. Forgiven? Yes. Seriously impaired? Yes.

Others who never get hooked on drugs still don't avoid the consequences. Jim is typical. He grew up in a Christian home. When he was sixteen he began experimenting with marijuana and alcohol. He never became addicted, but he's still paying the price in consequences years later.

He learned to chemically control his moods rather than deal with reality. It was risky to ask a girl for a date. She might refuse, and he would feel bad. But he could puff on a joint and feel good—every

Remember this very simple but powerful truth—one day you will be what you are now becoming.

time. So, while other teens his age were learning, through trial and error, how to deal with reality, he was puffing joints or drinking beer.

Later, when he turned 23, he decided to leave the shallow world of drugs and go back to real life. The problem was that he couldn't go back into life at an age-23 level. He had to go back at an age-16 level where he had stepped out. While others had progressed and matured, he had not. While they were risking and learning, he was not. He was using chemicals to control his moods. He now felt out of place. He had missed some important passages on the way to maturity.

Jim married a Christian girl, and they have three children. He has been unable to get and keep a good job. His spiritual life has been like a roller coaster ride. Now his wife and children have left him, and, he's miserable.

He had come to his senses all right, but too late. He had missed too many important steps. He will suffer the consequences of his trip to that distant country for the rest of his life. And so will all who love him.

Others form relationships while in the distant country that cannot be reversed. Many marry a mate that may not choose to leave. Others are divorced. Some may be pregnant or have children.

Once there was a fly that buzzed around a nice new piece of fly paper. He smelled the delicious smell. He thought of how nice it would be to have it all to himself. So, he landed on the fly paper. Holding one fist in the air he yelled defiantly, "My paper!" Then he noticed that he was hopelessly stuck. After it was too late, he discovered he was trapped. It was then that the fly paper smiled and said, "My fly."

The point is, you can't unscramble eggs—or lives. Sin, that we thought would be a delightful servant, becomes our master.

Not Everyone Is Capable of Forgiving

In Jesus' story the father represents God. He is capable of forgiving perfectly. Others often cannot.

Bill was a deacon in the church. He had a delightful family, but he began to get involved in drinking with some guys after work. After a while, and far more quickly then he expected, he became alcoholic. He began treating his family abominably when he was drunk. He wife stuck by him. For years she loved, she cared, and she waited. Finally she broke. She clenched her teeth and told him to get out. He begged her to give him another chance. She said she already had. He promised to do better. She said, "I don't care."

Now he's sorry. He has truly repented and has straightened out his life. He has lived a responsible, faithful, Christian life for six years. She still says, through clenched teeth, "I don't care!" And she refuses to have anything to do with him. She will not budge.

Is she wrong to be unforgiving? Yes, she's wrong. But is she still unforgiving? Yes, she is. Tragically, everyone cannot simply forgive us and run to welcome us back as the father in Jesus' story. Bill's story can be multiplied many times over.

Too Many Unanswered Questions

Also, there are too many unanswered questions about how the boy in the parable did when he got back home.

Did he stick with it this time? What about all the unhealthy habits he had picked up in the distant country? Was he *now* able to submit to his father's authority that he once thought was so oppressive? Was he happy with the "dull" life back home? Did *they* readjust and trust him? What about a prospective wife; how would she view his adventure? Did they want to accept him back?

Summary

From where I live, if you get on Highway 99 and go north you will come to the city of Fresno—*every time*! That's where Highway 99 leads. The dumbest thing I can think of is for a person to go to Highway

99, turn north and say, "Boy, I hope I don't come to Fresno."

A teen's life will be fantastic or tragic depending on what he does with it. He needs to look at who he is, what he is for and where he is going. There's only one way to live life that makes sense—the Father's way. You can have a fulfilled life in your Father's house, or an empty one in the pig pens of life. It depends greatly on how you look at it.

Remember this very simple but powerful truth—one day you will be what you are now becoming.

Questions for Thought and Discussion

1. What is different in the way parents are viewed by a typical six year old and a typical sixteen year old? Give examples.
2. Do you agree that teens must question authority? Explain.
3. Do you agree that most people who go into the "distant country" never make it back? Why?
4. What have you experienced that helped you grasp the fact that life is fragile, even for the young?
5. Why do so many young people from good families decide to go into the distant country?
6. Why do so many fail to ever come to their senses and return to their father's house?
7. What did the author mean when he said, "We can always be released from the guilt of sin, but we still must deal with the consequences?"
8. Give examples of people you know who went to the distant country and came to their senses too late.
9. Is it harder to make it successfully through the teen years today than before? What new traps are in the distant country to ensnare us?
10. Do you know of instances where someone truly returned from the distant country, but someone at home would not forgive him and welcome him home?

CHAPTER 9

Fitting into the Church

How do you view the church? What is it? Where did it come from? Why is it here? What is its purpose?

There are many concepts or views of what the church is and what it is for. Your view will determine the relationship you have with it. It depends on how you look at it.

Need for Clear Goals

In a previous chapter we noted that there is no worthwhile activity without clearly defined goals. We must have a known purpose. We can't get anywhere unless we know where we are going.

When we decide to take a trip, we don't simply get in the car and start off in any direction. We begin by deciding on our desired destination, then we chart a specific course that will get us there.

At each end of a basketball court there is a goal. Suppose that someone sneaked into the gym just before the big game and stole the goals. The theft isn't discovered until minutes before the game is to begin. There isn't time to get new ones; so, they decide to play the game anyway. No matter how skillful the play, no matter how much dribbling, passing, or fouling, the game will end with the score being zero to zero. It doesn't make sense to play a game of basketball without any goals. It makes less sense to live a life, or have a church, without clearly defined goals.

We often set "nothing" as our goal. Then we achieve it with remarkable accuracy.

Jesus said, "If thine eye be single, the whole body is full of light" (Matthew 6:22). James also said, "A double-minded man is unstable in all his ways" (James 1:8).

Activities Must Be Focused on the Goal

Once a clear goal is established, we then must focus our activities in that direction. Otherwise, we're not setting goals, we're merely making wishes.

We've all been in meetings where a decision is made about a particular issue. However, no one was assigned to follow through with the decision, and no specific steps to accomplish it were outlined. Unsurprisingly, nothing gets done.

When is a hospital not a hospital? Suppose, in your community they construct a new hospital. You know that the goal of any hospital is to make sick people well. You visit the hospital. There are some nice parking places near the entrance, but they are reserved for doctors only, and you have to search for a parking place far away. That's normal. You enter and see nurses scurrying about, doctors with stethoscopes looking serious and patients in clean beds. Nothing unusual here. You smell that antiseptic aroma that is unique to hospitals (which I think they just spray around to scare people). Everything is still normal. Then you discover that 95 percent of the people who enter that hospital die within a very short time. Would you want to go there as a patient? Of course not. No matter how it looks or smells, and no matter what the sign says out front, if it doesn't make sick people well it is failing. That, alone, is its goal.

Suppose, again, that in your community they construct a new shopping center. A merchant rents a space to open a shoe store. His goal is to sell shoes for a profit. During the grand opening he decides to give away free balloons to the children to entice

We often set "nothing" as our goal. Then we achieve it with remarkable accuracy.

customers into his store. The first day he gives away two hundred free balloons, but he sells no shoes. He works hard at giving away balloons, and within four months he breaks his best record by giving away over 500 free balloons in one day, but he still sells no shoes. Is he a success or a failure? He's a failure. Why? Is it wrong to give away balloons? No, but that's not his goal. That's not his purpose.

If we succeed at hundreds of *other things*, even good things, and fail to meet our goal—we have failed!

The Goal of the Church

What is the goal of the church? What is its purpose? Why does it exist? Your view of its purpose is exceedingly important.

Jesus established the church for a purpose. We should look to Him to tell us what that purpose is. The church is to fulfill the will of its founder, Jesus.

Well, what was His goal? Why did He leave heaven, come to earth and do all He did? He tells us succinctly in Luke 19:10: "The Son of Man has come to seek and to save that which was lost." That's what He said He came for, and that's the task He has left for us—seeking and saving the lost.

Jesus did not describe the church as primarily a worshiping institution. He described it as primarily a penetrating institution. He said it's like yeast. The basic nature of yeast is to penetrate the loaf. If you have a lump of dough and put some yeast in one end of it and leave it overnight, what happens? It penetrates. During the night it quietly, but steadily, permeates the entire loaf. The next morning you can take a pinch from any place on the loaf, and you'll find yeast. That's what the church is to do. You establish the church in a certain place, and it will quietly but steadily permeate that entire community. If you come back in a couple of years and go down any street, you'll find Christians. That's its nature.

Jesus says the church is like light. The basic nature of light is to penetrate darkness. Therefore, the purpose of the church is to lovingly, effectively, and boldly penetrate the world by communicating the good news about Jesus.

Importantly, it is not the task of the church to force, coerce, or trick people into responding to the gospel message. It is simply to communicate clearly. The Apostle Paul said, "Christ did not send me to baptize, but to preach the gospel" (1 Corinthians 1:17). We present the good news. The integrity of others is respected, and they are free to accept or reject Christ.

The classic description is that the church exists by evangelizing as fire exists by burning. Evangelizing is not what the church does because it's commanded—

It Depends on How You Look at It

evangelizing is its basic nature. The church can't help but tell the good news.

Many churches have lost sight of their fundamental nature and basic goal. We are constantly tempted to get off track and focus on lesser goals. But if we succeed at a thousand *other* things, even noble things (such as having inspirational assemblies, developing

> *Prayerfully and carefully find your own special ministry and pour your life into it. Give it all you have! Then don't worry about everything else.*

a loving fellowship, relieving suffering, feeding the hungry, building buildings, filling busses, having Sunday schools, and all kinds of other *good* things) and fail to reach our goal—we have failed! We fail our Lord who gave us the goal. We fail ourselves by not being what we were designed to be. And we fail all those who remain outside of Christ because of our neglect.

The goal, the basic nature of the church, is to communicate Jesus. That is why we exist. Everything we do should contribute in some clear, definite way to achieving this goal.

The church where you are, and your life in it, can become all it was designed to be. Or it may be something less. It depends on how you look at it.

How Do I Fit in?

The Bible teaches that we are individually reponsible to live before God according to our own unique potential. We are each to discover our own gifts.

Then we develop our personal ministry based on our gifts.

No two people are the same. My ministry will not be the same as yours. Things you do well, that are natural to you, that you easily get excited about, would be hard, unnatural, and difficult for me. So, you discover your ministry (whatever it is) and then give it your best shot. Meanwhile, I will do the same. And "whatever you do, do it heartily" (Colossians 3:23). Neither of us should wait around, expecting someone else to find a place for us.

Specialize

Once we have discovered our gifts, we can know what good ministries to get involved in and what good ministries we should not get involved in. In any active church that understands its purpose there are many more jobs that any one person can possibly

> *Jesus did not describe the church as primarily a worshiping institution. He described it as primarily a penetrating institution.*

do. If you are trying to be involved in everything that's going on, you are unnecessarily frustrated. And you are not being the best servant of the Lord that you can be. You need to specialize in your area of effectiveness.

Jesus is our example. He specialized. He refused to get involved with even good things that kept Him from His primary task. Once a man asked Him to be the judge in a grievance he had with his brother. Now, there's nothing wrong with being a judge. It's a worthwhile and noble thing to do, but that was not what Jesus came to do. So, He refused. "But He said to him, 'Man, who made me a judge or arbiter over you' " (Luke 12:14)?

On another occasion the people wanted to make Him their king. There's nothing wrong with the king business. It is honorable. (There just isn't much chance for advancement.) But it wasn't what He came to do. So, He refused them. He specialized in seeking and saving the lost. That was his goal from which He would not be distracted.

The apostles specialized, too. The first church fuss is recorded in Acts chapter 6. It was solved by the apostles telling the upset members to choose some other men to do the tasks they wanted done. The apostles said, "But we will devote ourselves to prayer and to the ministry of the word" (Acts 6:4). They specialized and taught others to specialize, too.

Prayerfully and carefully find your own special ministry, and pour your life into it. Give it all you have! Then don't worry about everything else.

Your potential to be a great servant of God does not depend on your age, your economic level, your nationality, your education, or other such things. It depends entirely upon your faith in God and your willingness to be used by Him. God wants you now—just as you are!

You can hold back, be uninvolved and unsuccessful, and blame others. You can get overinvolved, try to do everything, and be frustrated. Or you can discover and develop your special gifts, then use them in specific ministries to the glory of God. It depends on how you look at it.

Questions for Thought and Discussion

1. Discuss some of the ideas that people have about the nature and purpose of the church.
2. What is the primary goal of the church?
3. Name some things that churches often do that pull them away from their primary goal.
4. What aspect of the church's nature is Jesus picturing by using the illustrations of yeast and light?
5. What did Paul mean when he said, "Christ sent me not to baptize, but to preach the gospel" (1 Corinthians 1:17)?
6. Whose responsibility is it to see that you find a ministry?
7. Is it possible for a person to be overinvolved in church ministries? Explain.
8. What do you think is the major reason many people find it difficult to become healthily involved in church ministry?
9. How does discovering your special gifts help you know what ministries to avoid? Can you think of examples of someone in the wrong ministry?
10. Give examples from the Bible of specializing in ministry.

MY LIFE WITH GOD

CHAPTER 10

Seeing What God Is Doing

J. B. Phillips wrote a delightful little book entitled *Your God Is Too Small*. In this book he describes many inadequate views that people have of God. To some God is the Kind Old Man Upstairs, to others He is the Resident Policeman, and to others He is the Cosmic Killjoy dreaming up ways to rain on everyone's parade. Phillips' point is well made. *Whether* one relates to God, and *how* one relates to God, depends upon his *view* of God. It depends on how you look at Him.

Count Your Blessings

As we view God as the sovereign ruler of the universe and the giver of all blessings, it will be quite natural for us to be grateful to Him. As we count our blessings, we include the free gift of salvation. (It's a fantastic comfort to know that my place in heaven is certain.) We also include the blessing of a daily relationship with the Lord. We list our families, our health, and our relationships with others that bring us so much joy.

Is that all we have received from Him? Didn't we receive some pain? Didn't we receive some distress?

Didn't we receive some heartache? Didn't we receive some things we didn't like and would never have asked for?

Let's not make the mistake of viewing God as the giver of only the things we like and Satan or some other source as the giver of the things we don't like. Jesus said that God "causes His sun to rise on the evil and the good, and sends rain on the righteous and the unrighteous." Our Father knows that we need all kinds of things—both pleasant and painful. And, by His wisdom and love, He provides both.

The gift of food would not be appreciated without the gift of hunger. There would be no refreshment in the gift of cool water unless there was first the gift of thirst. Unless one knows something of loneliness, he cannot adequately enjoy the richness of friendship.

The Apostle James tells us that *"every* good thing bestowed and every perfect gift is from above, coming down from the Father of lights" (James 1:17). He also instructs us to "consider it all joy, my brothers, when you encounter various trials, knowing that the testing of your faith produces endurance" (James 1:2-3).

Grateful for All Blessings

Should we be grateful for *all* the gifts we have received from our Father, or just the ones we like?

In our culture we have the tradition of giving showers for newlyweds. It's a wonderful tradition because they need so much and have so little. Martha and I received enough sheets or towels at our showers to last 10 or 12 years. We are still using the toaster given to us by Al and Dorothy Krikorian almost 33 years later.

It Depends on How You Look at It

After the shower and the wedding, the bride sits down to write thank-you notes. Before her are all kinds of gifts. There are many wonderful, needed, useful gifts that she loves. However, she received three blenders. Is she grateful for all three? And there are all those run-of-the-gift-shop items, like the blue salt and pepper shakers and the yellowish-green candy dish that she will never use. Should she send thank-you notes only to the givers of gifts she liked? No! That would be unthoughtful and rude. She is to strive to be truthful and gracious but gratefully acknowledge them all.

What does the Bible say about gratitude? That is, should we be grateful for all our blessings or just for the ones we enjoyed? "Always giving thanks for *all things* in the name of our Lord Jesus Christ" (Ephesians 5:20). "In *everything* give thanks; for this is God's will for you in Christ Jesus" (1 Thessalonians 5:18).

The apostles give us an excellent example of praising and thanking God for even the negative gifts. They were arrested for preaching Jesus. "After calling the Apostles in, they [the Council] flogged them and ordered them to speak no more in the name of Jesus,

Unless one knows something of loneliness, he cannot adequately enjoy the richness of friendship.

and then released them" (Acts 5:40). That was certainly a "blessing" they could do without! That is something they would never have requested. How did they view it? How did they respond? "So they went on their way from the presence of the Council, *rejoicing* that they had been considered worthy to suffer shame for His name" (Acts 5:41).

Linked to Maturity

Actually, all this is related to maturity. Your maturity level will determine how you view things. And your view will determine your response.

A small child is not naturally grateful. He must be taught. He receives something he likes, and in his flush of pleasure and anticipation, he forgets to say thank you. Or he receives something he doesn't like and sees no reason to say thank you. How many times do parents say, "Now what do you say?"

The small child is ungrateful because he has no idea of the way things are. He has an incorrect view of reality. He is ignorant of receiving a gift. When he arrives in this world all of his needs are met automatically, it seems. He gets food without asking for it. It just appears. Whenever he is wet and uncomfortable, someone seems to automatically know it and takes care of it. Water, air, warmth—it's all just there. He has no concept that someone is striving diligently, often with sacrifice, to provide those things. Parents, therefore, spend much time and energy trying to help young children see life as it really is.

Older children move to the next level of gratitude—that of being grateful for what they enjoy. This, too, is inadequate and for the same reason. They don't see things as they really are. How many times have teens heard the lecture that begins, "Now, when I was your age . . . ?" Why do parents insist on saying that? Children have to understand that they are trying to tell them something. Parents want children to know that things haven't always been this way. It isn't automatic. Someone caused it. And children need to know that so they can be appropriately grateful. A mark of maturity is gratitude.

As we mature we learn to be grateful even for the painful experiences. But that usually comes later—not at the time. I can look back on times when my dad spanked me—an experience specifically designed to be unpleasant! At the time I was extremely ungrateful, to say the least. Now, however, I am so very thankful that my parents had the maturity and the wisdom to discipline me, even when it was very unpleasant for both of us.

The Bible states the principle clearly in Hebrews 12:11: "All discipline for the moment seems not to be joyful, but sorrowful; yet to those who have been trained by it, afterwards it yields the peaceful fruit of righteousness."

Once a little four-year-old girl had been naughty. For punishment her parents made her eat her supper at a little table by herself instead of with the family. Before she ate they suggested that she should say a prayer. As they stood around her little table she bowed her head and said, "Thou preparest a table before me in the presence of my enemies." Her gratitude would have to wait until later.

Summary

The depth and the richness of your relationship with God depends on your spiritual maturity level. It really depends on how you look at it.

Some people, like the small child, are unaware that their blessings come from God. They walk on His earth, breathe His air, and enjoy life and health from Him. Yet, in their ignorance, they believe that these things are just automatic. They don't know that they are caused by Someone. Therefore, they are ungrateful and have little or no relationship with the Giver of all their gifts.

Others, like the older child, recognize that the blessings they *enjoy* come from God. For those pleasant experiences they are grateful. Their relationship with God begins to deepen.

Still others, more mature, realize that *"all things work together for good to those who love God and are called according to His purpose"* (Romans 8:28). They have a rich, stable, unwavering relationship with God. They see His hand in all aspects of life. They feel His presence with them in the valleys as well as on the mountaintops.

You can learn to say with Paul, "I have learned to be content in whatever circumstances I am" (Philippians 4:11). It depends on how you look at it.

Questions for Thought and Discussion

1. What are some inadequate views that some people have of God? What are the results of these views?
2. What were some of your views of God when you were a child? How have your views developed?
3. Name some of the blessings that you enjoy most.
4. Can you name some blessings that you did not like and did not want but now see their value?
5. Discuss the ramifications of the statement, "The gift of food would not be appreciated without the gift of hunger."
6. Why could the apostles rejoice when they had been flogged?
7. Share some of the "when I was your age" stories you have heard (or told). Why do parents tell these stories?
8. Name and illustrate the three levels of maturity and how they relate to gratitude.
9. Is your relationship with God more precious to you when you are on the mountaintop or when you are in the valley?

CHAPTER 11

God at Work in My Life

When Christians receive great blessings and victories, they praise God for His goodness. When they encounter problems and difficulties, they turn to God for help. They understand that this is far more than the power of positive thinking. They are looking to the real living power of the real living God at work in their lives. They constantly pray for themselves and for others, trusting that God hears and will answer their prayers.

All Christians agree on the fact that God works in their lives. However, they disagree on *how* He works in their lives. Consequently, many are confused as to what they should ask for and what they can expect. Again, the way we look at it has significant effect on our lives.

If we expect too little, we will ask for too little and miss many of His blessings. The Bible warns, "You do not *have* because you do not *ask*" (James 4:2). On the other hand, if we expect too much and ask for something He never promised, we will become disillusioned when it doesn't happen. The Bible also warns, "You ask, and receive not, because you ask amiss" (James 4:3).

I think it is helpful to recognize that there are three ways that God chooses to work in our lives.

Direct Intervention

Sometimes God simply chooses to intervene directly. When He does, it defies human explanation. God is sovereign and can choose to act in His world any way He chooses. When this happens we often say He is working *providentially*.

Note these promises from the Bible:

"Ask and it will be given to you; seek and you will find; knock and the door will be opened to you. For everyone who asks receives; he who seeks finds; and to him who knocks, the door will be opened.

Which of you, if his son asks for bread, will give him a stone? Or if he asks for a fish, will give him a snake? If you, then, though you are evil, know how to give good gifts to your children, how much more will your Father in heaven give good gifts to those who ask Him!" (Matthew 7:7-11).

"I write these things to you who believe in the name of the Son of God so that you may know that you have eternal life. This is the assurance we have in approaching God: that if we ask anything according to His will, He hears us. And if we know that he hears us—whatever we ask—we know that we have what we asked of Him" (1 John 5:13-15).

It should be noted that this providential care of God in the lives of His children is not the same as the special miraculous gifts which were given to reveal and confirm of the Word. These were usually called "signs and wonders." They were received in a special way, given for a special purpose, and for a special time.

Still, God works. He is alive and well. He works in His world. When a child is sick, when a relationship is hurting, when problems arise, we implore God for His help. Sometimes He simply intervenes and brings the healing or the solution we desire. Praise Him!

But He doesn't always choose this response. After all, He is not a Genie in a bottle. We must not forget that we are His servants, He is not ours—to be ordered around by us.

In Cooperation

Sometimes God chooses to act in cooperation with natural forces and processes.

The scriptures give examples of this. In Luke 10:34 the Good Samaritan used the medicinal properties of oil and wine to help the injured man. In James 5:14 elders are directed to use the medicinal properties of oil—along with their prayers. In John 9:6 Jesus used spittle and clay as He healed a blind man.

God works in cooperation with medicine, doctors, nutrition, counseling, etc. We, too, must work in connection with these known principles. There is little point in glibly asking God for healing from lung cancer if we continue to smoke. It does little good

There are times when disease, accidents, trials, heartaches, or losses are given, and they are not going to be taken away—not providentially, not in cooperation with other things, not at all. They must be endured. Yet, they do not defeat us, and it does not mean that God has forsaken us.

to pray for God to heal my marriage while refusing counseling and continuing a selfish attitude toward my mate. It's futile to ask God to help me lose weight while I continue poor nutrition. Why should I implore God to make me more mature in Christ and help me overcome some besetting sin if I am not willing to work in cooperation with Him to bring about the desired result?

The story is told of a neighbor who drove up to a farmer's house and announced that the dam had broken and the flood waters were coming. He offered the farmer a ride in his car to safety. The farmer refused, saying, "The Lord will take care of me."

Later, when the waters began to rise, a rescue boat came along. He refused to get in, saying, "The Lord will take care of me."

Still later, as he sat on his housetop to avoid the rising waters, a helicopter arrived to take him to safety. He still refused, saying, "The Lord will take care of me."

Alas, he drowned! After death he asked the Lord why He didn't save him from the flood. The Lord said, "I did. I sent you a car, a boat and a helicopter, but you refused my help."

Rick and Renee Thomas discovered that their delightful toddler, Simon, had leukemia. They felt the pain that only comes to parents in such situations. They did two things. First, they, and the church, were persistent in prayer asking God for Simon's life and health. They also entered an intensive and aggressive medical program which included three years of chemotherapy and another five-year maintenance program. Simon's leukemia is now in remission. He is eight years old and as normal as apple pie. Was his healing from God? You bet it was! They not only prayed diligently, but also worked in cooperation with known medical procedures.

The blind man's healing with spittle and clay was no less from God than the leper He healed with a touch. Simon Thomas' healing is no less from God than if it had been instantaneous. They are simply different ways that God chooses to work. In either case God is to be praised!

Grace Sufficient

There are also times when God chooses not to alter the circumstances that face us, but He gives us

> *You see, it's not the facts that determine real success or failure in life; it's the focus! The fact is, it depends on how you look at it.*

wisdom, strength, and grace sufficient to deal with it. There are times when disease, accidents, trials, heartaches, or losses are given, and they are not going to be taken away—not providentially, not in cooperation with other things, not at all. They must be endured. Yet, they do not defeat us, and it does not mean that God has forsaken us.

God's people have often had to deal with unimaginable persecution. Where was God? He was still there.

In Romans 8:35-39 Paul (who himself endured much persecution and pain) lists tribulation, distress, persecution, famine, nakedness, peril and sword as things Christians would be called upon to face. And he adds, "but in all these things we overwhelmingly conquer through Him who loved us."

Paul himself three times prayed to God to remove some affliction which he called a thorn in the flesh. The Lord did not remove it. He said, instead, "My grace is sufficient for you." Paul understood this and, instead of feeling forsaken, said, "I am well content with weaknesses, with insults, with distresses, with persecutions, with difficulties, for Christ's sake; for when I am weak, then I am strong" (2 Corinthians 12:8-10).

Even Jesus prayed in the Garden of Gethsemane, just before his crucifixion, "Let this cup pass from me." He did not want to have to suffer the terrible pain of the cross. God did not remove the cross—but He did give Jesus the strength to endure it.

This third way of responding is still from God and is a valid form of His care for us. When certain trials come and will not change, then we must allow them to change us. They are to be used for our strengthening.

If we are aware only of God's working through direct intervention or in cooperation, then we will become disillusioned when God responds in this third form. And that can be faith shattering. If we understand that at times the healing touch of God takes the form of grace sufficient, we can be open to receive it and grow from it.

All children with leukemia are not like Simon Thomas. John Claypool had a beautiful daughter, Laura. At age 8 she was diagnosed with leukemia. He prayed for God's intervention. He worked closely in cooperation with doctors. Eighteen months later, Laura died.

John struggled, he grieved, he agonized. Then he began to allow God to help him to creatively accept what he could not change. He learned that *all* of life is a gift. He wrote, "Everywhere I turn I am surrounded by reminders of Laura—things we did together, things she said, things she loved. In the presence of the reminders, I have two alternatives—either to dwell on the fact that she has been taken away or to focus on the wonder that she was given at all."

In our lives we often have the same two alternatives. And our response will be determined by the way we look at it. We can dwell on the fact of the loss, or we can focus on the wonder that it was given at all.

We will be called upon to face the loss of loved ones, perhaps children. Our children may move away or leave the Lord. Some will face devastating rejection—divorce. Some will lose a boyfriend or girlfriend to another. We may lose our precious health. When disastrous things happen in life—and they will—we can choose to dwell on the loss and hurt, or we can focus on the wonder that it was given at all and allow God to give us healing, comfort, and victory!

Summary

These three forms of healing from God are summarized in Isaiah 40:31: "They that wait upon the Lord shall renew their strength, they shall mount up with wings as eagles, they shall run and not be weary, they shall walk and not faint."

We all will face dark and difficult times. Sometimes God responds by direct intervention and simply solves it for us. At those times our hearts sing, and we mount up with wings as eagles. We praise God! Sometimes God responds by working in cooperation with natural processes. Then we can run and not be weary. He brings healing, and we thank Him for His care. Sometimes He doesn't remove the problem but gives us grace sufficient to deal with it. And all we can do is walk and not faint. Then we focus on the gift and, again, thank Him for His grace.

You see, it's not the facts that determine real success or failure in life; it's the focus! The fact is, it depends on how you look at it.

Questions for Thought and Discussion

1. How does prayer relate to the power of positive thinking?
2. What difficulties arise by expecting too little from God?
3. What difficulties arise by expecting more from God than He promised?
4. Name three ways God works in our lives.
5. Tell of instances where you believe that God intervened and worked providentially in your life.
6. Give examples of situations or teachings where God was seen as if He were a genie in a bottle.
7. Give examples of God working in cooperation with natural forces to bring healing.
8. Give examples of people who desired one result but acted contrary to, instead of in cooperation with, natural processes.
9. Give examples of people who allowed God to give them grace sufficient for their difficulties and were strengthened.
10. Give examples of people who did not allow God to give them grace sufficient and were damaged or stuck in an unhealthy response.
11. Do you agree, after this study, that real happiness is not based on the facts of life but rather your focus on life? Comment.